GRAHAM CRACKS
Turning Beer into Literature
One Joke at a Time

By Richard Neil Graham

San Diego, California, USA

Published by LA NY Edit

Dana,
I couldn't have written this without you! ☺ All the best!
Richard N. Graham

Copyright © 2015

No part of this book may be reproduced, stored in any retrieval system, or transmitted by any means; electronic, mechanical, photocopying, or otherwise; without the prior written consent of the publisher.

Graham, Richard Neil, 1958-
Graham Cracks:
Turning Beer into Literature
One Joke at a Time

Printed in USA by CreateSpace
ISBN-13: 978-0983406099
ISBN-10: 098340609X
LCCN: 2015910121

Cover Design by Michael Graham
Back Cover Design by Breck Wilson
Front cover photo by Bradley J. Fikes
Front cover Photoshop by Rigel Morrison

TABLE OF CONTENTS

Acknowledgments: 4

Author's Note: 5

Foreword: 6

Just the Facts: 11

Politics Schmolitics: 86

Burning Questions: 100

Antisocial Media: 109

Unsportsmanlike Conduct: 117

Wimmen: 134

Alco-Haul: 150

The Theory of Relative-ity: 159

Use a Pun, Go to Jail: 162

Overheard: 168

ACKNOWLEDGMENTS

Many thanks to my cousin Michael Graham for designing the front cover; to Breck Wilson for designing the back cover; to my *old* friend Bradley Fikes for the front cover photo; and to Rigel Morrison for his Photoshop skills on the front cover. It ain't easy making me look good.

Thanks also to Jackie Carpenter-Krieger, Laurie Grimaldi, Karen Horne, Nancy Lane, Ryan Malethe, Chris Shamrell, Jimmy Vivona, Denise Wilson and other friends who liked my jokes and encouraged me to keep writing them down.

Very special thanks again to Karen Horne for writing the foreword to this weighty tome. You're pretty funny, too!

(And thank you, Harbor Town Pub of San Diego, for the friendliness of your staff, the fun and the liquid inspiration!)

AUTHOR'S NOTE

I started posting these jokes as Twitter tweets in about 2012, where they got absolutely no traction. I couldn't understand how even dumber jokesters than me had thousands of followers, when I had 27, so I eventually moved my jokes to Facebook, where they caught fire... or at least smoldered a little bit.

Many jokes that I'd originally written have been deleted. One, which I thought was a Pulitzer Prize winner – "What do you call it when your lizard escapes from his terrarium? A reptile dysfunction." – had been stated in similar form at least three years before I came up with it.

Other deleted jokes were just too stupid, too topical, or so "not politically correct" that I'd become a pariah if they were published. The ones that are too stupid, topical or not politically correct enough that remain are my errors alone.

FOREWORD

My friend Rich wrote a book. Until he did, I wasn't sure he even had a command of the English language, what with him being born in Canada* and all, and the hockey thing. I hear you get hit in the face a lot.

So imagine my surprise when he started posting some of these *Graham Cracks* for his Facebook friends/guinea pigs to laugh at, and we *did*. They were genuinely funny. And some of them were both wise and funny. A few were even true and funny, though to protect his pride, I won't tell you which those are.

From the time I first met him I recognized that Rich Graham was a unique character: Intelligent, witty and soulful; a deep thinker, a horrible dresser and the kind of real friend his own friends can count on to come through for them.

But to actually *sell* a book of funny, one has to be creative as well, and damned if he wasn't. I started collecting my favorites from his very first posts, and was amazed at how clever many of them were. Reading them made me realize my friend Rich was practically *brilliant*, definitely way smarter than he looks.

So, instead of wincing inwardly when he said he was going to publish them, as one usually does when a friend is about to make a humiliating mistake, I was pleased for him and actually thought it was a great idea. So if you don't like this book, it's probably partly my fault.

While I'm being honest, I should also tell you that I think he mostly wrote it to help him pick up girls, and I only agreed to write this foreword so I could get a bunch of free copies to show off to my family.

Just buy the book already. It costs less than your Yuppie breakfast at Starbucks and you won't regret it, especially when you hear laughter coming from your guest bathroom, where you stashed it so your friends could read it while they were otherwise occupied.

Karen Horne
The Frozen North (Washington State)
December, 2014

*As everybody knows, Canadians only speak Canadian. That's sort-of like English, only you have to say "eh" after every sentence, and apologize a lot. And some Canadians only speak French. Don't get me started on that.

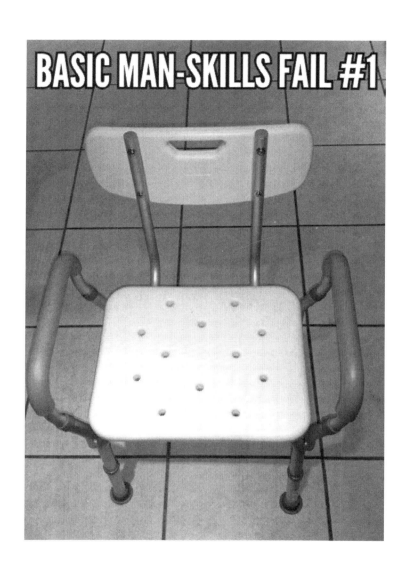

JUST THE FACTS

Things that only very young and very old people say with pride: "I just PEED!"

If Deep Purple's "Highway Star" had been released right *after* I'd received my driver's license, I'd be dead right now.

I'm not a very fast runner, but I bet I could set a personal record in the mile if I was chased by a bear.

Monday is the root of all evil.

When I hear the word "bipolar," I think of bisexuals in the Arctic.

If I got laid as often as I think about getting laid, I'd be too tired to get laid.

Grammar Nazis are a drag, but if you abuse the English language, your going too here form me.

There's nothing but beach in Phoenix. No ocean, but tons of beach.

Know why your argument stinks? Because you pulled it out of your ass!

Whenever I hear the word "condo," I think of condoms, because I know that *someone* is getting screwed.

In the old days, stagecoach bandits stole the savings of banks' customers. Now banks do.

Death and taxes. And pee. You gotta pee.

The people laughed at Mrs. O'Leary's cow. The people laughed till she said, "Burn."

In my career, I made $100 minion dollars! OMG, I wish I could spell!

Hey, I'm texting here! Why can't you watch where I'm going?

Whoever put oatmeal in cookies forgot the purpose of dessert!

I got up early once. I looked around; and then I went back to bed.

My belt broke and my pants fell down below my butt. I'm finally fashionable!

Got a fortune cookie today that read, "Your dream will come true." It had a date on it. It had expired the previous week.

Now that I'm in debt, I finally know why they call it Chase Bank.

Playing the harmonica with a mouthful of crackers sucks *and* blows.

Hearing Deep Purple's "Space Truckin'" as elevator Muzak elicits feelings of outrage mixed with, well, outrage.

Living right means spending all your cash; maxing out your savings, checking and credit card accounts, and *then* having your wallet stolen.

"Hate" is a strong word. I'd say that I loathe or despise clowns, but I don't hate them. Their big shoes? Those I hate.

Jimi Hendrix' latest album is better than anything Tupac's put out since he's been dead.

Priorities seem skewed when you can puke in public, but you have to hide to pee.

According to NBC, thieves recently made off with 21 tons of cheese. I'd sure hate to be around when it's cut.

I was going to have a sex-change operation, but I didn't have the balls.

No one knows I'm famous, because I shun publicity.

One good thing about today's terrible pop music is that it gets me out of bed in the morning to throw the radio out the window.

People say that I'm easily amused. Well, it's cheaper than cable!

Whoever said revenge doesn't taste sweet had no taste buds.

When I was a kid and looked up at the ceiling, I saw all sorts of neat things. Now all I see is a stupid ceiling.

A buddy at the dock broke two propellers. So I gave him props.

Only ugly people should be television news anchors. That way, the only people who watch would be people who actually care about the *news*.

That's kinda creepy, #1: When male spectators at golf tournaments shout at the ball to "Get in the hole!"

She don't lie, she don't lie, she don't lie... propane.

Some people tell me I'm too passionate. %×¥€!!! those robots!

Someone just said, "Nip it in the butt." My inner grammar detector went haywire!

Couch for sale. Worth $300 new, has been in storage one year. Selling for $1,750.

Overly emotional men make me weep.

In high school, I was voted most likely to exceed... common sense, boundaries and the speed limit.

Solar power is the future. Therefore, I copyright the sun. I win!

Potty humor stinks.

Terrorists don't scare me half as much as my mom did when she'd say, "Just wait till your father gets home."

Little yappy dogs with Napoleonic complexes should go back to France, where they came from.

If you want to cross the street in front of my car, just let me know. I won't run you over if I don't even *know* you.

Today, while visiting San Diego State, I truly was a Big Man on Campus. All right, Fat Man on Campus. Semantics.

I'm like a potent pharmaceutical: 4 out of 5 doctors recommend taking me only in very small doses.

So many ugly people; too much time.

When I see a dual-seat baby stroller with only one child in it, I want to yell out, "You've lost one!"

I refuse to buy Swiss cheese because you don't get everything that you paid for.

One good thing about slamming on the brakes is that it clears things off the front seat. Sorry, Mom.

What do you call a well-educated dinosaur? A Thesaurus.

Ever wonder why the ocean is salty? Ever peed in a pool?

I felt proud to have written and published a book. Then I thought, "Snookie."

We drivers could get somewhere on the freeway if we could only blow up all the damn Priuses.

Shins are like masochists; they seek out pain.

Irony: Companies shrink the text on instruction manuals while the only people who read them are losing their eyesight.

If you can't beat 'em, ridicule 'em.

Want to keep thieves from breaking into your car? Cover your valuables with books.

Pepperoni has never let me down.

I had to throw a prostitute off my boat last night, so I gave her the old heave ho.

It is better to mistake a gopher snake for a rattler than vice versa.

I think everyone should be named Adam or Eve. Then there'd be no confusion when meeting new people.

I'm going to turn this damn laptop into the world's most expensive Frisbee!

I get a bit crazy when I think of all the psychotherapists I've kept in business.

Never yell at your neighbors when you're in a porta-potty. They could exit first.

Today, guys get together and form boy bands. Back in my day, we were the sultans of *schwing*!

Getting older means sleeping a lot… and *liking* it.

When someone darts out into the street between two cars, I rudely yell, "How did you live so long?" If I hit them, I politely say, "Sorry!"

Photo by Yves Rubin

Mistakes I Didn't Make:

I never broke up a marriage, or ruined a happy home.
I never told Willy Shakespeare that I was master of the poem.
I never dropped a Stradivarius on a hard concrete floor,
Or told Oprah's fans that her TV show was a bore.
I never broke Clapton's fingers, shaking his hand with my monster grip.
I never shot a man or put a hole in a sinking ship.
I never told Muddy Waters that he didn't pay his dues,
And I never dreamed of telling B.B. King that he hadn't lived the blues.
I never told Wayne Gretzky how to shoot a puck,
And I never told the IRS that I didn't give a damn.

Remember that time Einstein made a smooth move? Man, that was *hilarious*!

I think it's really mean to make fun of people's looks... at least until they have more money than you.

I wouldn't sell my soul to play guitar well, but I would sell my conscience.

I'm really a very agreeable person if you don't contradict me.

If you find an unpaired sock *and* it has a hole in the heel, it's mine.

It's a shame that Richard can be shortened to Dick when all the real dicks are named Peter.

If I only had a dollar for every time I said, "If I only had a dollar."

Lottery tickets, you are very close to wearing out my eternal optimism.

It's true, I don't sleep. Not because I'm a vampire. Because I'm too sexy for my bed.

Judgmental people suck.

Know why superstitions are stupid? There's no superstition for *Monday* the 13th. I rest my case.

Simply keeping an enemy from getting what they want is as sweet and satisfying as any form of revenge.

Back when I had a job... well, forget about that. No one cares about ancient history.

Waiting for the bus reminds me of how much I hate waiting for the bus.

They say that we should count our blessings, and I do: I am not a big fan of graffiti, but the wannabe gangstas who scratch their signs into toilet seats do provide butt grip.

It's 11 p.m. on April 14th and I'm doing my taxes. There's no way I'm going to wait till the last minute *this* year!

Rich people can never know the absolute satisfaction of getting the last little bit of cracker crumbs and salt from the bottom of a Saltines' crackers plastic sleeve.

The only thing worse than people who don't signal is people who never turn it *off.*

Instead of "God damn it!" how about saying "Mankind damn it!" That's probably a lot more accurate.

Sadly, after all I have learned in life, I must admit something shameful. I am a hater. I know it's wrong, but I really, really, really despise stupidity.

An honest American businessman is now as rare as a nun with a tan line.

My "To Do" List: Stop war. Stop polluters. Start Department of Peace. End cancer, depression and alcoholism. Do the damn laundry.

I always arrive at the doctor's office late to give him time to get back from golf.

It's not fair: When I was young and skinny, my savings expanded. Now I'm old and fat and my savings shrink.

It's funny how old blues music makes me happy, but today's new music gives me the blues.

I may be old, mean and cranky, but I'm at least I'm no curmudgeon – I don't have a lawn!

I'm not going to hell in a handbasket; I'm going to Limbo in a lunch box.

When I was a kid, snap, crackle and pop went my breakfast. Now, it's my back and joints.

God is a comedian that most people don't get.

When I was young, love made my knees go weak. Now my knees are weak and my loves... just go.

Getting fat has compensations – do you know much lint you can collect in your belly button? I just made a sweater!

Want to learn patience? Let old people drive you somewhere in their car.

Money is just a tool, but some tools have too much money.

Living on a boat is a microcosm of living on land. Creatures that live below may never bother you, but those who live above *will* shit on you.

Some gamblers live in a pair a dice.

I don't like the profanity in music and movies. I know all of those words and can fill in the blanks all by myself.

When I'm around dogs too long, I want to be around people. When I'm around people too long, I want to be around dogs.

**10 Good Things about
Living in a Cave**

Stalactites and stalagmites make
great conversation pieces,
and they're free!
If you back up against the rear wall,
nothing can sneak up behind you.
Many people will mistake you
for a wise man.
There's no need to keep up
with the Joneses.
Solicitors might be eaten
by wild animals.
No chirping smoke detectors.
No upstairs neighbors.
No Internet spam.
No landlord.
No rent.

The bus driver can be an hour late, but if you don't get on in a hot second, *you're* the asshole.

In a pinch, manly men know that a toothbrush is a good stand-in for a mustache comb.

Good News: Drinking Mountain Dew does *not* cause a man's testicles to shrink. Bad News: Now I have to buy bigger shorts.

As a comedian, you're not successful until someone steals your material. No one steals my material.

I'm all messed up with nowhere to go.

I am waiting for the awesome day when bacon is used as currency.

When annoying guests are coming over, place boxes of stuff on all the available places to sit. They'll stay for a while, but not long enough to drive you crazy.

It's annoying when your 86-year-old father mocks your haircut, after he traumatized you for life by cutting your hair when you were a kid.

Even if you're innocent, it's always better to see the cops before they see you.

I am surrounded by gays and lesbians. Fortunately, they all respect my choice to be heterosexual.

You can't believe in both God *and* astrology. Well, you can, but if you do, you're kind of screwy.

Never trim your nails just before you have to change the battery on your cell phone.

Here's a new phrase you can use during the holidays: "Happy Everything." It's trademarked, so you will have to pay me to use it.

When you haven't been wise, apologize. When you've been wronged and you're right, fight!

The burden of being the last sane person in America weighs heavily upon me.

Real men don't get pedicures. They wait until their toenails fall off and regenerate themselves. Smart *and* cost effective.

I was feeling deathly ill, so I walked *really* slowly past a medical-marijuana dispensary several times.

I was wrong once and I deeply regret it.

Not all bosses are assholes. All of *mine* were, but not all bosses are assholes.

It's not fair that black people get to name all the cool stuff like rap, twerking and hip-hop, but I get no credit for rapcrap and hipless.

Fake military names that are probably not wise to use in your serious novel: Private Property, Major Mayhem, and Colonel Colon.

You can't wear your heart on your sleeve when you're wearing a T-shirt.

Aristotle said: "Nature does nothing uselessly." Mosquitoes? I rest my case.

All of my heroes are dead, but it's not my fault.

On national holidays when I didn't have to work, my job wasn't too bad at all.

My current goal in life is to be a 50-year overnight success.

In World War II, a cat survived three different warship sinkings. That would only be a big deal if it had survived 10.

The sky? It's up to me.

I used to get angry when my computer crashed. Now I think it's telling me that multi-tasking is for the birds. Thank you, computer! I'm going out to watch the sun rise!

Never throw anything away. It ain't me, but somebody wants that shit.

I was so thrilled when my buddy told me that his wife was going to have a baby. "I'm not shooting blanks!" I yelled, and then I ran like hell!

I hate it when all of the magazines at my doctor's office are for funeral homes.

Viagra and Cialis are always advertised while golf is on TV. That's why I refuse to golf – just in case erectile dysfunction is communicable.

Live long enough to become a burden to your parents… twice!

When a dude with no socks took his shoes off in a crowded subway car, I got a little foretaste of hell.

With all of today's corporate mergers, I don't know if Purina still owns Jack in the Box... so I don't know if I should eat my burger or feel good about feeding it to my dog.

I don't ask much of technology, but when my mind works faster than my computer, I know that it's time for an upgrade.

Best recent Optical Character Recognition errors: Employer = craplover. First = Fink. Administrative = Anus:itift, See = Pee. Gotta love technology!

Street crime in Los Angeles shrunk measurably for four hours the other day. Justin Bieber was being searched by customs agents at LAX.

When I sing karaoke, the audience makes requests. For instrumentals.

Every single generalization is false, except this one.

Old age has definitely arrived. I just called my friend's dog "Leon." Louie was like, "What the hell, dude?"

I'm so embarrassed! I was doing my laundry, but forgot that I wasn't at home. I was in front of the dryer in a chair, naked, having a beer, when the cops walked in.

Some people are addicted to drugs, others to food, still others to sex. I am addicted to hockey, but not necessarily in that order.

I occasionally put typos in my writing on purpose to make people with low self-esteem feel better about themselves.

One of the great mysteries of our time: Figuring out exactly where the Los Angeles Times hides the Sunday comics.

Welcome to California. Just don't bring in any fruits. Hey, don't yell at me. It's not *my* rule!

If I hand you my phone, it's to show you what's on it. Don't touch the screen until I give you permission to touch the screen!

When I make a mistake, I admit it. Don't just stand there; this could take a while.

After smacking my head on cabin beams, tripping and stubbing my toes on halyards and cleats, and having my hands burned and torn by ropes, I finally understand why I love sailing: I am a frickin' masochist.

I am one of the sanest men I know. This scares this shit out of me.

What Not to Do When Drunk

Pontificate on politics or religion, especially if there is a tape-recorder or camera in the vicinity.
Cut your hair.
Try to impress anyone.
Do anything around a swimming pool.
Tell your boss what you think about him.
Talk back to policemen or bring up the subject of donuts.
Talk back to your mom.
Talk back to your mom, *especially* if she's a cop.
Tell the bartender that he reminds you of a dwarf from The Hobbit. Post anything on Facebook
Oh yeah... drive.

OMG! I thought I had gone blind in one eye, and then I realized that a lens had dropped out of my glasses.

This guy called me passive-aggressive, so I shot him. But I used a silencer.

I stay up late night after night, just wondering why I'm tired all the time.

What Johnny Cash did to his son by naming him Sue was terrible. I'm going to call my son a *man's* name: Cracker.

Thank heaven for the Statute of Limitations!

Whenever someone tells me, "You have no idea," I wonder what they are talking about.

I had a job once; I didn't like it.

I wish the postman would just take the mail straight to the recycling bin and save me the trip.

All humans are psychos. The key is to find the psycho who best fits your needs.

Sunrise is the most sublime part of the day. So I've heard.

A real man admits his fears. I fear cheese mites.

Every time I hear "Cat's in the Cradle" I feel guilty about not spending enough time with my cats.

Please don't argue with me about literature. I didn't read thousands of books to compete intellectually with people who can't read a stop sign.

Global warming *is* a conspiracy, and I admit it. I left my oven on for several decades. My bad.

I can't understand why I can't lose weight. I take a brisk walk to the liquor store every day.

Sometimes I say, "What is my purpose on this earth?" Then I say, "I didn't *ask* to be born!" Then I say, "Well, who the hell did?!" Then I shut up for a while… but not for very long.

Living on the edge in the 21st century means texting in a Jacuzzi.

I've eaten Monterey Jack cheese my whole life, but I never wondered who the hell Jack was until tonight. Somehow, that creates feelings of guilt. But then I eat some cheddar, and I am good again.

There are worse things than high-pitched screaming babies on the subway. You could be in an airplane.

Fun with math? Are you kidding me? The only time I had fun with math was when the bank made an error in my favor.

We need more guns! You can't eat food! Wait, I got that wrong...

I cannot believe how many things I find to complain about! Let me think of a blessing... Well, I'm a gud speler!

There is one thing I have never been able to figure out. In what month should a man take his annual shower?

The other night, I had a Twinkie for the first time in about 40 years. I got such a sugar rush that I said, "Hallelujah!" and threw away all my cocaine.

Never let anyone tell you you're not funny…. looking.

I saw a "Baby on Board" placard today for the first time in years, and I thought, "Isn't that simply an invitation to kidnap?"

Well, yes, I did promise you a rose garden, but I never expected you to hold me to it.

Maybe some people are homeless because they simply cannot take one more word of bullshit from the people they've lived with in houses.

Humans are the only species that give high fives. That's because other animals don't play sports.

Life is like a box of chocolates. Typically, rich people are eating them while you look at them through a window when you're freezing just outside.

Highway signs that say "Airplane Patrolled" crack me up. Have you ever been pulled over by a cop in a plane? Ha ha! That said, I still get a lot of tickets on the highway and I can't figure out why.

I only have two, and you're on my last Achilles' heel.

When I left my last job, my co-workers threw a huge party for me. Unfortunately, it celebrated my departure and I wasn't invited.

I cleaned my house once. Worst decade of my life.

Did you hear about the video game player who was kicked out of his friend's basement? He went Wii Wii Wii all the way home.

I forget if my bed has memory foam.

"Fashion" cracks me up. Anyone who's *hot* will look good in *anything.* Levi's and white T-shirts, people. That's fashion.

My credo is that everyone should have a mission statement.

I was an English major in college, but I have never understood why it is supposedly incorrect to end a sentence with a proposition.

When I make love on a golf course, I expect a hole in one.

Every fisherman needs a catch phrase.

ATM fees are banks' way of thanking you for saving them tons of money on human tellers.

Take the letter "a" out of the alphabet nd you hve lphbet.

American corporations' greatest export: Jobs.

I can never remember if it was Alexander Graham Bell or Sherlock Holmes who said, "Watson, come here I need you."

I am always looking for a town called Cognito so I can honestly say, "I am in Cognito."

God told me to start a new religion. There was only one commandment: I can't tell anybody the details.

She may have been green with envy, but at least she was environmentally conscious.

A child prodigy, I was always 20 years ahead of my peers. Envious, they all now claim that I am just as old as they are.

Air guitars sold here. Cheap. All sales final.

OK, OK, I admit it: I am bipedal. Now get off my case, you Homosapienaphobe!

I love cop porn... I mean popcorn!

Except for a few humongous gaps, I know everything that there is to know.

I could not find any cheese in Quebec, just a poor substitute called fromage.

This morning while washing my hair in a sink, I finally figured out where the Flock of Seagulls' lead singer got his hairstyle.

If you put on makeup to walk from the bathroom into the kitchen, you might just be overdoing it. This goes for you ladies, too.

There is no scarier body of water than the Erie Canal.

I recently cooked Jiffy Pop Popcorn with a cigarette lighter. It took a week, but I didn't burn *one* kernel!

What do traffic, aging and babies all have in common? They suck.

It is said that you fear what you don't understand. I fear men with pony tails.

I like it when people cut me off in traffic. It shows that they trust me.

If you trip over things in your own house, you might have *too much stuff!*

Sadly, and unfortunately for the world at large, I believe I may be running out of time to become a teen idol.

What is the epitome of English literature – Monty Python's The Cheese Shop or Hamlet's soliloquy by Shakespeare? That is the question.

I just took a 90-day road trip and didn't have one argument. It's not me. It's you.

If you spend a lot of money on perfume, consider taking a bath or a shower instead. You too, ladies.

You say I'm not green because I'm driving my father's Lincoln Town Car? Are you kidding? I carry a Cooper Mini in the trunk!

It sure would be nice if tourists wore "I don't speak your language" T-shirts. It would save a lot of hassles.

I didn't pass all of my college courses on the oil industry, but I certainly did pass Gas.

Hey radio DJ, unless aliens have landed, nothing you can say is important enough to speak through the beginning or ending of a song.

Alzheimer's rock and roll: "There's a certain girl I've been in love with a long, long time." "What's her name?" "I don't remember."

A gas station going out of business is like Paris Hilton winning an etiquette contest. It should be impossible.

I want the name of the jerk that made the eye of a sewing needle narrower than a piece of thread.

My advice to couples considering divorce: Please try to stick together. No one really wants to deal with either of you separately.

I am no judge of coffee, but I've never been disappointed by a Mocha Frappuccino.

I'm mad and I'm bad, just like Justin Bieber. (Apologies to the late John Lee Hooker.)

I don't get the concept of speed bumps. I speed like the signs tell me to, and the bumps wreck my car's shocks!

I thought I'd lost my cell phone, but it was only my mind. Thank God!

Dear cell phone companies: I do *not* like surprises happening in my pocket. Thank you.

When you find out what you finally want to do with your life, don't let anyone stop you. Well... except maybe a SWAT team.

A while back, I decided to be extremely annoying. Once again, I have proved to be very successful in meeting my goals.

I don't need to work out. I get enough exercise just opening the security packaging on my electronics purchases.

If drug usage continues to mushroom in America, I can see the names of future housing subdivisions: Crackhead Estates, Green Grass and High Times Condos, Methamphetamine Manor.

One day, I couldn't find anything to complain about. I had to pinch myself to see if I was alive.

It's not nice when mean people call me names… like "unemployed," for example.

Another reason a boat is better than an apartment: In a boat, the downstairs' neighbors may attack you, but they'll never complain to the management.

It ticks me off when people get mad at me for taking naps in restrooms.

"Weird" is a relative term. Be yourself. That's real. "Weird" is just a name that cowards will call you.

Snoring is not a crime. But if you snore when I'm trying to sleep, I *will* kill you.

Little League parents are the Tea Partiers of sports.

I'm looking for a specific woman to marry so that I can hyphenate my name to Graham Crackers.

I had to quit my job. I couldn't take another bored meeting.

What's a nincom? It's a nincompoop with constipation.

This stuff about interstellar space, gravity and black holes? It's way over my head.

Religious wars make as much sense as heavenly penitentiaries.

Want to quickly determine if someone takes himself too seriously? Carry around a Whoopee cushion.

The thing I hate about conspiracies is that no one ever includes me.

Mamas, don't let your babies grow up to be morons who don't cover their mouths when they cough.

On your birthday, do as I do. Dance naked in the moonlight to the universe's song. Just make sure there are no cops around.

Hey, you, jerk on the subway with your little bag on the seat next to you. There's an elderly lady standing right next to you who could use a seat! I'd give you a piece of my mind… if you weren't the Rock of Gibraltar in tennis shoes.

I don't always know what's right, but I usually know how I feel. And I feel that you're a jerk.

Twins have double standards.

It was cool yesterday to get birthday wishes from Germany where it's already tomorrow today. I was so busy that I didn't know that today was my birthday yesterday until I received that call from Germany's tomorrow. I just made myself dizzy.

Greed is a very powerful religion.

Terrorists don't frighten me as much as tourists who carry their umbrellas at eye level.

The Flintstones were so ahead of their time on LGBT issues. The show's theme song stated: "We'll have a gay old time."

I have great friends, wonderful acquaintances… and a few assholes that entered my life when I wasn't looking.

Note to self: Do not text while walking alongside a cliff. You could trip and faaaaauuuggghhhhh….

God's major failures are his creation of humans and... *give me a minute!* ... Mosquitoes.

Comedians do us a world of goof.

I am a renaissance man and I speak several languages – English, American, Canadian and un poquito Spanish.

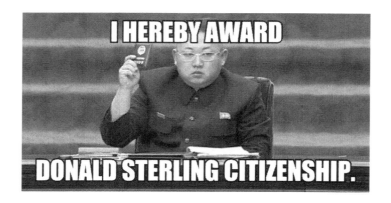

POLITICS, SCHMOLITICS

What Wall Street financiers say at parties: "We earned money the old fashioned way; we *stole* it."

Fox News: Because even idiots need news.

Barack Obama is *not* black. He's golden.

Earth Day: Busiest day of the year for polluting corporations' public relations departments.

Most American presidential candidates are toast before they even get out of the bread bag.

I like guns as much as the next guy, but carrying them into WalMart? That's just small dickishness.

I am running for President.
To see my campaign platform,
please go to
www.DontPanicIGotThis.com

I'm guessing that the politicians who despise the 1960s never got any free love.

"Trickle Down" = Rich people peeing on my head.

My response to hateful right wingers who trash immigrants: Remember the U.S. government's broken treaties with Native Americans and quit yer whining. You don't know how good you've got it.

America needs its women to stand up and be Koch blockers.

Lush Rimbaugh only exists because of our weakest instincts.

The Civil War was not civil, and it's still being fought by America's dumbest politicians.

Fight climate change or lose Florida? Tough call. Very tough call.

A compassionate conservative is a Republican who cares deeply and truly about himself.

A Libertarian is a Republican with no conviction.

"The rich are better and smarter than you and me." Midas, Donald Sterling, Donald Trump. Thus, I refute.

What do Hansel and Gretel have in common with political campaigns? They both leave a trail of crumbs.

Religion: Don't ask, don't tell.

If right wingers are so conservative, what, besides their own money, are they conserving? It certainly isn't the environment.

If right wingers are right, I want to be wrong.

Many left wingers are assholes, but it's so more fun to bug right wingers. They go bat-shit crazy when you use two simple tricks: facts and logic.

It used to be fun to make fun of politicians, but now the joke's on us.

Hell no longer accepts telemarketers. However, there is still plenty of room for parking-enforcement officers and people that drive slowly in the fast lane.

I was not always so negative about politics. I was pretty naïve, in fact. I thought that America ran itself pretty well, overall, and that you had to be smarter than me to be president. Then George W. Bush came along and I said, "What the hell?"

I try to be as politically correct as possible, but I draw the line at "cavepersons."

Another great thing about NSA surveillance on U.S. citizens? I no longer have to take notes.

Sometimes I hate myself. Then I think, wait a minute, Congress exists!

I use the NSA as my own personal cloud.

I'm gonna mess with Facebook's and the NSA's data-mining programs and "like" both the Tea Party and Obama at the same time.

From a future "What Goes Around, Comes Around Department" – "I'm sorry, sir, but we don't serve white heterosexual men."

I'd rather be a heathen with a heart than a "Christian" without one.

Creationists are right. Dinosaurs *did* live alongside humans. Unfortunately, Noah did not realize that dinosaurs subscribed to "Don't Ask, Don't Tell," and many a Sidneysaur was actually a Cindysaur.

Bullies are to courage as politicians are to truth.

Voting against your own interests is like paying someone to beat you up.

There's a phrase, "Crazy from the heat." Add "and humidity" and it explains why the American South fought the Civil War.

I was born in Canada and am a U.S. citizen, so when people celebrate the War of 1812, I'm very conflicted.

You have the right to make mistakes. Just make them when I'm not around, OK?

Kim Song un – Paris Hilton's brain and Jeffrey Dahmer's heart.

Democratic politicians are terrible. Republican politicians are terribler.

You say that you want a vibrant U.S. economy without 30,000 handgun deaths a year in a society that doesn't glorify violence against women while being Puritanical about sex at the same time? You're gonna have to move.

BURNING QUESTIONS

Did you know that trees are both vegetables *and* vegetarians?

Why would anyone put something called sham*poo* on their heads?

To the guy on the freeway who just cut me off without signaling: Who do think you are, Kanye West?

Isn't it interesting how many more handicapped drivers there are when you're trying to park at a sporting event these days?

Do dogs ever bite their own tongues?

Are man boobs sexier to men or to women?

If God exists, why are there still mosquitoes?

Why are people who *don't* text while driving such crappy drivers?

Why the hell do they call it a Q-Tip?

If Obama was born in Kenya, how come he's not a long-distance runner?

Why can't scientists take nose- and ear-hair genes and transplant them in our scalps?

Have you ever noticed how people who become sports mascots suddenly get bigheaded?

If we call a spy a mole, do moles call miners spies?

Who is Megan Doppler, and why is she always talking about the damn weather?

"A River Runs Through It" sounds like a great movie. I live in Los Angeles. What's a river?

Shouldn't gardeners use leaf *suckers*, not blowers?

How will we know when Duck Dynasty has jumped the, um… duck?

Since 90 percent of the cars on the road are as ugly as hell, why not cover them in Michelin-Man outfits and save some lives?

What's so "conservative" about cutting down a forest to build a mini-mall?

Trying to be helpful, you tell someone to get off the subway at the wrong stop by accident. Does that make you a *bad* Samaritan?

If volcanoes are caused by gas deep inside the earth, what causes earthquakes? Constipation?

Hey, Australian pal, how's it going in Upside Down Land?

What if you were asexual and went through life without knowing what you were missing? Wouldn't that be *awesome?*

It's not surprising to see sick people at the hospital, but where do all the ugly people come from? Is there a shortage of plastic surgeons or something?

News Flash: "IKEA recalls 17,000 portions of moose lasagna after finding traces of pork." Is that physically even possible?

As state slogans go, "Pure Michigan" is pretty lame. Really? As opposed to what? "Sleazy Wisconsin"?

Remember when Bitstrips were cool? Me neither.

So many men are dressed as women these days, at least on the subway. Is that where the phrase "going underground" comes from?

I am outraged. I know the economy is bad, but have you *seen* the cost of a penile reduction?!

I paid for anger management classes from Tiger Williams, relationship tips from Tiger Woods and health advice from Tony the Tiger. Why am I still so screwed up? Grrrrr!

People see me online late at night all the time and say, "Go to sleep!" I say, "You have a job, what the hell are *you* doing up so late?!"

I've gained a lot of weight over the last couple of years, so I was thrilled yesterday to be able to see my feet! Yeah, I was wearing swim fins. What's your point?

Ever notice how announcements on the subway sound just like Charlie Brown's teacher?

Isn't it better to be crazy and harm no one than to be "sane" and make everyone around you miserable?

Photo by Bob Makela

ANTISOCIAL MEDIA

There's one sure way to find out who your true friends are: Send 'em Facebook game requests.

I don't have a television, yet I know all about Fox News, Kanye West, moronic politicians and Honey Boo Boo. It may be time to drop the Internet.

The fewer Instagram followers you have, the more honest you are.

To the guy I know who put "Facebook" as a new "skill" on his LinkedIn account: You. Will. Never. Get. Hired.

I like Facebook and Twitter, but I *love* InstaGraham.

You're going to have to Kik me in the Vine before I get into any more social networking sites.

Facebook is a great way to find out which friends you hate. Never "friend" your probation officer on Facebook.

I got 30 days in the hole from Facebook. I friended too many people. I feel so ashamed. Not.

I have an unfair advantage over 90 percent of Facebook's users. I can spell.

I never really knew what an asshole I was until I joined Facebook.

I was InstaGraham before InstaGram was cool.

Twitter is on-the-spot, late-breaking news. Instagram is cool photos. Facebook is puppies, kittens and full-on war. GrahamBook will combine all three social media sites.

People who post too much on Facebook are total pains in the .... ah, never mind.

My buddy Randall's idea of living dangerously is to record the game, and then go on Facebook, hoping that no one tells him the score.

Why doesn't Facebook create a social media site for adults?

Sometimes, when I am attacked on Facebook for my perceptive commentary, I feel like a gorgeous woman. Don't hate me because I'm brilliant.

C'mon cell phone battery, just let me finish one more twe

If I send you a game request on Facebook, it means that I either love or despise you. Search your soul for the answer.

Hey Facebook friends. I don't "do" pokes. It's not you, it's me.

Shooting fish in a barrel is like correcting grammar on Facebook.

Twitter's 140-character limit enforces creative workarounds, unexpected haiku, sharpened self-editing skills and English-major rationalizations. If you are a moron, the character limit doesn't matter, does it?

My father despised Facebook. I think he was on to something.

I choose to fight on Facebook with morons. I am smarter, but they have the numbers, *I've* been the moron.

YOU MIGHT BE ADDICTED TO FACEBOOK IF…

You used to wear out the knees of your jeans, but now it's the butt.

You never leave your mother's basement, except to get a new modem.

You use Facebook to order pizza.

Facebook is the only reason you have a cell phone.

You've served 30 days or more in Facebook solitary confinement.

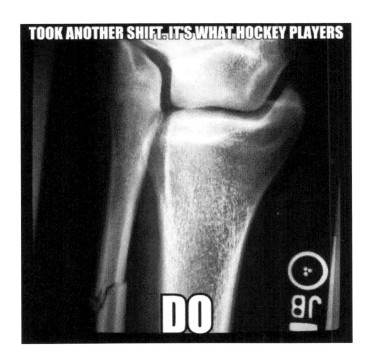

UNSPORTSMANLIKE CONDUCT

I refuse to join the organ donor program. I can't take the chance of saving the life of an Anaheim Ducks fan.

Johnny Rivers has a new song about the Los Angeles Dodgers' hot prospect from Japan, whom the team is keeping under wraps: "Secret Asian Man."

Swimming is fun until you're swimming by accident.

The best song for penalties in the National Hockey League: "The Man in the Box."

I would not be a boxer for any amount of money. I'd be too dead to enjoy it.

I hate those fair-weather ice hockey fans that leave after the second quarter.

What happens when a NASCAR race winner is lactose intolerant?

Four out of five dentists surveyed recommend playing hockey.

Corey Perry rhymes with dairy, and I am lactose intolerant.

What is an Olympic shuttle driver's ethical dilemma? When Team Germany offers you cash to run over Team France.

I was exhausted after golf today. I refuse to carry the golf cart on my back anymore. It's a stupid rule and I don't see *anyone* else doing it.

What did the polite hockey player say to his opponent before they fought? "One lump or two?"

Hug a man with black eyes or a broken nose. Hockey players need love, too.

People who hate hockey don't appreciate that it gives violent men a civilized outlet for their aggression.

I love how ostensible Los Angeles Kings fans give up on their team at the first sign of distress. I use the word "ostensible" because I know that those morons don't understand that word *or* ice hockey.

The San Jose Sharks' theme song is Dionne Warwick's lesser-known tune, "Do You Know the Way to the Golf Course?"

I hate it when I get kicked out of Honda Center for wearing a Toyota jersey.

I have no slap shot, can't skate, am old, take too many penalties, have bad knees and a bad back, can't take a check and hate referees on principle. Man, do I ever love hockey!

Why do I only follow one sport closely? I only have so much time to hate so many teams' fans.

In the middle of a Kings/Sharks Stanley Cup Game 7, I ran down to a computer shop to get my father's laptop fixed. Does that make me a good son… or a poor Kings fan?

Ducks are evil and live in Anaheim!

Be kind to all people. Not everyone is smart enough to be a Los Angeles Kings fan.

"A duck's quack doesn't echo, and no one knows why." I know why. It's just like Dracula who can't see himself in a mirror.

It's pretty sad when the "Fan of the Game" at Honda Center is wearing a Los Angeles Kings jersey.

Hockey politics: Puck Futin.

What's the big deal about a no-hitter? I played baseball for years and got no hits.

I think the entire Donald Sterling saga boils down to this: Despite all of his money, he still couldn't get laid.

Being a Los Angeles Kings fan is not the pinnacle of life. However, it *is* better than being a fan of any other National Hockey League team.

Wayne Gretzky has scored more often than Justin Bieber has been arrested.

The woman I'm looking for will be like the Los Angeles Kings... without the 44-year losing streak.

After hockey the other night, a buddy grabbed my left boob. It wasn't sexual, but I figured out one reason why women hate it. It hurts!

Hockey is the world's greatest sport. Others claim that distinction for football, baseball, basketball and soccer. Others are wrong.

If Katy Perry wore nothing but an Anaheim Ducks tattoo, I still wouldn't hit on her. I am a Kings fan. I have my standards.

I can't wait until I finally get to the Pearly Gates and learn that playing hockey really *is* the meaning of life.

European soccer players dive more often than submarines.

What's the difference between a hockey game and a baseball brawl? In a hockey game, they throw punches. In a "basebrawl," they throw gloves.

When I saw a Rottweiler wearing an L.A. Kings jersey, I thought, "As long as he knows the difference between Canadiens and Canadians, we're good."

When I was a kid, my hockey nickname was "Boomer." I always thought it was because of my big slap shot, but tonight I had beans for dinner and I finally figured it out.

It you don't cheer for the Kings at home game because they are behind in the score, you might just be a Ducks fan.

The last time the Toronto Maple Leafs won the Stanley Cup, most of their current fans were in diapers. Next time they win, those fans will be in Depends.

News Flash: Several NBA players were recently rushed to hospitals with injuries ranging from broken toenails to bruises. After hearing the news, several hockey players died laughing.

I may not be a famous hockey player, but like players from the San Jose Sharks, Toronto Maple Leafs, Philadelphia Flyers and Columbus Blue Jackets, I am also out on the golf course in May.

When Wayne Gretzky was a child, he scored goals by shooting pucks through the legs of the chair that his grandmother was sitting on. I could have been as great as Gretzky if my family could have afforded a chair.

I look forward to the COSMOS episode that explains Anaheim Ducks fans.

One cold winter's night, I offered an Anaheim Ducks jersey to a homeless man to help him keep warm. He said, "I would never stoop that low." So, we used the jersey as kindling for a bonfire, and made it a win-win situation.

I once met Walter Gretzky, Wayne's father, along with two of his friends, Bob Coyne and Bob Bradley. Knowing that he was an avid golfer, I asked Walter, "What's your handicap." He said, "Bob Coyne."

A friend said, "NBC's hockey coverage is so bad; it's like they're talking to people who don't know anything." They are – Ducks and Sharks fans.

I have about 4,000 Facebook "friends." A good percentage of them are idiots, fanatics, psychos or Chicago Blackhawks fans. But I repeat myself.

Hey Advertisers: I think that a "lower-body injury" in hockey is an awesome advertising opportunity for Viagra.

WIMMEN

I'm psychic. At least, women *think* that I can read their minds.

Women laugh at me all the time. I thought women *liked* men who make them laugh.

I *like* the silent treatment.

Women are right about men and their fear of comitm, commitem, comitt, ah, screw it!

Remember when women threw away their bras to proclaim their independence from male dominance? I miss those days, too.

I am tired of being seen just as a sex symbol.

Is it considered impolite to tell a woman, "You look fantastic," and then ask how much her boob job cost?

I am down with dating a cougar, but unfortunately, for me, cougars are 80 years old.

A full moon always reminds me of the night my lover kicked me out. That's when I looked up to the second floor and saw her butt sticking out the window.

I was husband material when husband material wasn't cool.

Ladies, don't you just hate it when you trim your mustache and you go a little too far and one side doesn't match the other side? Me, too!

I had a date once.

I don't buy my love presents. I'm sure she wouldn't want me to cheapen our relationship by bringing money into it.

"I will give you everything I have!" I said. "You have nothing!" She replied. I will never understand women.

"When opossums are playing 'possum, they are not 'playing.' They actually pass out from sheer terror." Why this reminds me of dating, I don't know.

I hate it when women undress me with their eyes.

Regrets? I have thousands: All of the women I met in my life who had no taste in men.

My dad and I only clean house when female guests are arriving. With enough warning, we can do an entire year's worth of cleaning in about two hours.

Ladies, don't you just hate it when you're shopping for clothes and someone asks you how many months pregnant you are, and you're not pregnant? Me, too!

I hate to see women cry. I simply don't know how I'm going to tell all my lady friends when I'm finally out of circulation.

Mr. Bean taught me everything I know about women.

I find it hard to take women seriously who bitch about the toilet seat being left up, but who *don't replace the empty toilet paper roll!*

Women use words I've heard before but never understood. "Intimacy," for example.

When we were teenagers, my older sister once threw a heavy iron at my head and missed. If she had been accurate, I would be dead. How can you not love a woman like that?

Never tell a four-foot-tall woman that smoking will stunt her growth.

If I ever have a daughter, I know what I'll call her to keep teenage boys away from her: Ebola.

Why do women give straight men such grief? It's gay men who design their uncomfortable clothes.

Ladies, Super Glue makes a great clear nail polish, but it's murder getting your fingers separated afterwards.

If women's sunglasses get any bigger, they'll be windshields.

Women are strange. Fight a mountain lion for them and they yawn. Walk a mile home alone after 2 a.m. and suddenly, you're James Bond.

If you rap about hoes and bitches, don't expect to keep women in stitches.

Why are all the women I love already taken by lesbians?

Had I been more successful with women as a young man, I probably would have been married and divorced by now.

Please don't be like other women and laugh at my equipment. (Hey, I'm talking about my laptop!)

I never felt a generation gap until young American women began tattooing their chests. There are two gifts from God that *cannot* be improved by any amount of ink: Breasts.

Biologically speaking, women are animals.

I was shocked when my lady left me. "I thought it was the little things that mattered!" I cried.

I received visual confirmation today that women having their picture taken suck in their bellies just like men.

Modern women have their priorities all screwed up. They go for 6-pack abs when I offer a kegger.

If men sweat and women glow, you, lady, are a brightly lit fountain.

It is my personal belief that never getting married solves the problem of divorce.

Venus de Milo was a pacifist. How do I know? She couldn't bear arms.

The TV show Deadliest Catch is supposedly about storms, peril, frigidity and crabbing. I'm going to sue the show, because I know it's really about my wife.

Listening to a nagging woman is like frying bacon naked. The pain is intermittent and sharp, but it's not usually life-threatening.

Making a beautiful woman laugh is like making an angel sigh; life doesn't get much better.

One good thing about being a confirmed bachelor is that you can never be accused of cheating on your wife.

You know those laid-back buddies with scraggly facial hair that suddenly clean up, dress well and get professional photos taken? Blame a woman.

I have a guaranteed tarantula-free bedroom. Come on over, ladies.

Wouldn't it be funny to put a micro-cassette recorder in a baby stroller and have a kid's voice saying, "Help! Help! This is not my mommy!" No, I guess not.

Let me break it down for you. Men like pretty women. Pretty women like providers. Everything else is just noise.

Most women play hard to get and act uninterested in me. They are so cute!

"Inch by inch, everything's a cinch," is good advice, most women agree.

Ladies, when you change everything about your husband that you don't like, do you know what you get? A woman.

Gentlemen, only *you* can prevent cat ladies.

My Craig's List ad: "Single man. Married 17 times. Looking for wife. M*ust* supply references."

MY GIRLFRIEND IS SO HOT...

My girlfriend is so hot; the army wants to use her as a laser.

My girlfriend is so hot; the bar can't keep their ice from melting.

My girlfriend is so hot; she can weld without tools.

My girlfriend is so hot; the sun considers her competition.

My girlfriend is so hot; she can fry eggs on her forehead.

My girlfriend is so hot; she caused global warming.

My girlfriend is so hot; icebergs fear her.

My girlfriend is so hot; she goes in Jacuzzis to cool off.

ALCO-HAUL

Health advocates will tell you that you should drink 8 glasses of water per day. What they won't tell you is that beer contains water.

I am inspired by beauty... and alcohol.

You know that Coors Light advertisement where mountain climbers rush in with one or two frosty brews? Isn't that a bit cost-inefficient?

Sometimes, when it's very late, the stores are closed and I'm hungry, I rejoice that beer is food.

They say if you can "pinch an inch," you need to lose weight. Anyone got a pair of huge calipers I can borrow?

How about marketing all huge domestic American beers as shampoo? They actually do give body!

Another great thing about getting fat... when you forget to buckle your belt, your pants don't fall down.

Food poisoning is a crummy yet effective way to begin your weight-loss program.

Sadly, the members of my beer support group have become enablers.

I am not happy about getting fat, but there are compensations. Food can roll down your chest, hit your belly, pop up into the air and land right in your hand. Munch out!

I had to be rushed to the emergency room today after going to the beach. Apparently, I got a hernia from sucking in my gut.

Intellect is key... until you really, really have to pee.

It's tough being so incredibly witty after this much alcohol.

When dine-and-dash and beer runs are Olympic events, I'm in!

It's *not* a beer belly. It's an abs protector.

Beer is an ancient gift from the gods. It's legal, and the only real side effects are hangovers, a beer gut and a total lack of interest from women.

There's a song that states, '"In heaven there is no beer.'" I think that song smacks of Satanism.

I'm not an alcoholic. I'm just thirstier than most people.

Alcohol is not a solution. Wait. Actually, it *is* a solution, technically. But that's not what I was trying to say. Let me have another beer and think about it for a moment.

Scientists say that you are sexually frustrated if you peel labels off beer bottles. I only peel wallpaper, so I'm good.

To please some people, you have to *be* alcohol.

I am not simply drinking beer. I am also cleaning out the refrigerator.

I am so angry. I went on a liquids-only diet and gained weight! (The beer tasted good, though.)

I get a lot of grief for my beer consumption. However, if you were me and had to live with my brain, you'd drink, too.

I am *not* drunk. I am hops intolerant.

I drink beer to get the piss out.

I may be drunk... but you... well... you're... *sober!*

"Son," I said. "I want to teach you the difference between quantity and quality. Quantity is Anheuser Busch. Quality is almost any other brewery."

Starbucks coffee is responsible for more failed screenplays than alcoholism.

I'm a Belieber. I belieb I'll have another bier.

I love the sound of the ocean in my beer bottle.

I don't always drink beer, but when I don't, I am sleeping.

If I had all the money that I had spent on beer during my lifetime, I could probably buy a fairly large Pacific island. I'm quite happy with my choices, though. Unless that island had a brewery. Then I'd be pissed off.

SCHIZOPHRENICS

PLEASE DO NOT EXCEED 4 PEOPLE AT A TIME. THANK YOU!!

ANONYMOUS

THE THEORY OF RELATIVE-ITY

My Uncle Donnie once told me I'd make a good farmer, He said, "Rich, it's a big farm. Spread it thin."

Me: "Mom, Dad, I've decided to live on my own from now on." Parents: "That's just great!" Me: "So glad you agree! I've placed your luggage outside."

I could have been a genius if not for my ancestors and their crummy DNA. (Jerks.)

When you have sisters, who needs aliens?

As my aged father's caregiver, I use science and common sense to choose a proper diet. Since I've sworn by it for 56 years, I am convinced that pizza and beer is the solution. My dad? He can eat whatever the hell he wants.

My family is so gnarly, even the men snore!

My family moved from Toronto to Los Angeles in 1969. It took a while, but I finally tracked them down.

My father told me, "You're a pain in the ass 90 percent of the time!" Hallelujah! I'm improving!

Cousins are like having great friends without having to put in any effort to get them.

My grandfather, Grampie Nielsen, lived with us for a while. He made me mad by telling me what to do. One day, I said, "OK, Grumpy!" He laughed, and we were fast friends after that.

During the big Sylmar earthquake in 1972, Grampie yelled, "Quit shaking the bed!"

USE A PUN, GO TO JAIL

Supporting killer whales when you love dolphins simply defeats the porpoise.

Life's not fair. I don't smoke marijuana, but I have a pot belly.

Whenever someone farts in public, I try to have a rebuttal.

A stake a day keeps the vampires away.

It was a stark and dormy night at the college residence hall.

What the blanket maker said to the writer: "Make wove, not lore."

Why did the thief go to M.I.T. to steal a car? To get a *smart* car, naturally.

Sum peeple r 2 stoopid for werds.

I'm starting a book club for criminals called Prose and Cons.

There is won shore weigh too tell if people are reading yore online posts.

"Why are you wearing a pith helmet?" asked one elderly gent to another. "Going too senile," replied his friend.

I didn't fall out of my boat. I was pushed out. By Al Kohol.

The only super moon that I know is named Keith.

They say that puns are the lowest form of humor, but I think that theory has been spelunked.

Panda Express: Whom a veterinarian calls if a panda is about to give birth prematurely.

Why is spelling important? Because you never want to *wok* your dog.

If you must gamble, bet on driftwood; it's a shore thing.

How Oregon got its name: An Indian named Orr left the state. His buddy said, "Orr, he gone."

Ladies and gentlemen, please keep it clean. This has been a Pubic Service Announcement.

Some say that puns are the lowest form of Hugh Moore, but Hugh says it's actually Lee Moore Ricks.

Though I am strong, please don't take me for granite.

WHY I USED MEMES INSTEAD OF MY OWN DRAWINGS IN THIS BOOK

OVERHEARD

Overheard: "My teeth are from Mexico." - An old American sailor in San Diego.

"She runs like a fat girl." – My nephew Marcus

"I look at the obituaries every morning. If I don't see my name, I carry on." – My buddy, Anno Willison

I told a friend that I'd gone from covering inline hockey to writing about lingerie football. Sarcastically, she said, "That's a step up."

Who's playing at the Hollywood Bowl tonight?" "Some idiot's mother." "That's Yo Yo Ma, you buffoon!"

"I told my sister that I was dating this 'Rich' guy and she said, "How do you know? Did you ask him?" – A former girlfriend

"I can't be a good wingman while I'm carrying a purse." – Heard in passing

"Excuse me. Are you in my way?" – Nathan Price, editor, SportsTravel magazine

"I'd like to pick your brain for a moment, if you have one." – Phil Baker, ad sales, SportsTravel magazine

"Never get into a pissing contest with a skunk." – My father

"Your driver's license says you're 50! You said you were 38!" "Oh! I thought you asked me how old do I *feel!*" – Pawel, an old friend

Upon seeing a ball made of cheese: "That's eatable." "No, Marcus, that's edible." "It's a eat-a-ball!" – My nephew Marcus

After receiving a hug from a neighbor who asked why he wasn't in school: "That's OK, Mrs. Ricard. I have head lice." – My nephew Marcus

After seeing a fat platinum blond at the supermarket: "Look, Mom, Miss Piggy!" – My nephew Stephen

"If you are going to eat an elephant, take small bites." – My father

"Older women are the best. They give it their all, knowing it could be the last time." - Bob, a bartender at the Balsam's Hotel in Dixville Notch, New Hampshire

"I was going to buy you an ice-cream cone before you went and did that." – My mother

"I feel for you, but I can't quite reach." – My mother

"In arguments with my lady, I always get in the last word. 'Yes, dear. You're right. Yes, I know. Yes, yes, I'm *sorry*.'" – A man I met in Mexico in the 1980s

The one time I meet Pete Rose and he says to me, "Nice jacket. Who shot the couch?"

"To them, I'm invisible." – A middle-aged friend who likes to go to Starbucks to look at all the pretty young women

"She's got more silicone than the front end of a Corvette." – My cousin Scott Graham

"Can't open a new window until you close one." – My smart phone stole that line from my mom!

Once, a lady friend wanted me to see a movie with her called "Eternity." I said, "No way." When she asked why, I said, "Seems kinda long."

"What hamburger? All I saw was legs." – My father, after seeing the Carl's Jr. advertisement featuring Kate Upton

"You're not old. You're a young man in an old man's body." – Dan, a young traveler from England

"Oh my, oh dear, I'd be dead if I wasn't here." – My mother, according to my father, though I don't recall her ever saying it

Write Your Own Jokes Here!

Write Your Own Jokes Here!

Write Your Own Jokes Here!

Write Your Own Jokes Here!